Y0-BBF-759

MALCOLM CAMPBELL HIGH S
3400 NADON STREET
MONTREAL, QUEBEC H4J

MALCOLM CAMPBELL HIGH SCHOOL
3400 NADON STREET
MONTREAL, QUEBEC H4J 1P5

Visions of the Future:
Palm Reading

by
Elizabeth Hoffman

A **cpi** Book

From
RAINTREE CHILDRENS BOOKS
Milwaukee • Toronto • Melbourne • London

Copyright © 1977 by Contemporary Perspectives, Inc.
All rights reserved. No part of this book may be reproduced or utilized in any form or by any means, electronic or mechanical, including photocopying, recording, or by any information storage and retrieval system, without permission in writing from the Distributor and the Publisher. Inquiries should be addressed to the DISTRIBUTOR: Raintree Publishers Limited, 205 West Highland Avenue, Milwaukee, Wisconsin 53203 and the PUBLISHER: Contemporary Perspectives, Inc., Suite 6A, 230 East 48th Street, New York, New York 10017.

Library of Congress Number: 77-22207

Art and Photo Credits

Cover illustration and illustrations on pages 6, 12, 20, 22, 25, 30, 31, 32, 38, and 45, Isadore Seltzer
Illustrations on pages 8 and 46, New York Public Library Picture Collection.
Illustrations on pages 15 and 41, from "Witchcraft, Magic and Alchemy." by Girllot de Givry, Houghton Mifflin Company/George G. Harrap & Co. Ltd.
All photo research for this book was provided by Roberta Guerette.
Every effort has been made to trace the ownership of all copyrighted material in this book and to obtain permission for its use.

Library of Congress Cataloging in Publication Data

> Hoffman, Elizabeth, 1921-
>   Visions of the Future: Palm Reading
>   SUMMARY: Discusses palmistry, a method of predicting the future by interpreting the lines on the palm and fingers.
>   1. Palmistry—Juvenile literature. [1. Palmistry] I. Title.
> BF921.H7   133.6   77-22207
> ISBN 0-8172-1029-6 lib. bdg.

Manufactured in the United States of America
ISBN 0-8172-1029-6

Contents

Chapter 1
Jennifer and the Wet Palm   5

Chapter 2
Make Your Own Hand Prints   10

Chapter 3
Meet Some Hands   14

Chapter 4
Let Your Fingers Do the Talking!   18

Chapter 5
Thumbs Up   24

Chapter 6
The Shape of Things   28

Chapter 7
On to the Palms   34

Chapter 8
Life Lines and Head Lines   36

Chapter 9
The Unanswered Question   45

Jennifer and the Wet Palm

Jennifer's hands were wet. She knew they would be! It happened every time she was scared of something. And today she was scared.

Jennifer had heard about her Aunt Kate for years. But she had heard so many different things, that she wasn't sure that everybody was talking about the *same* Aunt Kate. To her mother, Kate was a "sweet woman who means no harm." To her dad, Kate was quite something else. "Your Aunt Kate," he would say, "may just be the smartest person I have ever known. She can tell you more about *you,* just by looking at your hands, than the ten best psychologists in the world."

Aunt Kate had spent the last 20 years traveling around the world. She had been to nearly every country and had met hundreds of rich and famous people. She had been invited to the homes of presidents and kings. She had worked with some of the best detectives in Europe and North America.

Why were these people interested in Aunt Kate? It wasn't just that she was "a lovely woman," as most people called her. It wasn't that Aunt Kate was rich or famous herself. She wasn't rich at all, and most people had never heard of her. But Aunt Kate did one thing that made her stand out: Aunt Kate was a *palm reader*.

For years, Jennifer had waited for Aunt Kate to read *her* palm. Finally the day had come. Kate was visiting her hometown and had promised to read Jennifer's palm right after dinner. "If you promise to wash all the turkey off your fingers," Aunt Kate cautioned with a smile. Now, as they finished dessert, Jennifer was beginning to have some second thoughts.

"What will she tell me about myself?" Jennifer wondered. "My hands look just about like *any* hands. I don't see anything very different about them. What if I don't like what I hear? What if she sees something awful in my future?" Her hands felt like *puddles* of water now, so she quickly wiped them dry with her napkin. She might just as well have saved herself the trouble, for when her aunt got up from the dinner table

Long ago, as well as today, people wanted to know their futures. The well-to-do visited gypsy palm readers who whispered secrets of the future to them.

and looked her way, Jennifer's hands were wet once again.

Aunt Kate walked toward the living room and Jennifer slowly followed. "How can anyone read a person's palm anyway?" she asked herself. Then, as if to calm her racing heart, she decided, "I don't know if I can really believe in this stuff!" But Jennifer knew, right down to her bones, that she was entering a world of mystery. It might be the most exciting adventure she would ever have. "Let me look at your hand," Aunt Kate said. Jennifer obeyed, lifting her hand and giving it slowly to her aunt. To her surprise, her hand was suddenly *dry*!

Aunt Kate began to read her niece's palm. "Sometime soon, you will receive a letter in a blue envelope," Aunt Kate read. "It will tell you about an airplane trip you will soon take."

Jennifer's mouth fell open in amazement. She couldn't believe what she was hearing. "Can you tell this just by reading my palm?" Jennifer asked with a puzzled expression.

Aunt Kate decided then and there to tell Jennifer all about the art of palm reading. We, too, can learn something about this unusual art which some people believe can predict the future.

Make Your Own Hand Prints

Wouldn't it be interesting if you could read messages in people's hands! Some people think this is impossible. Others believe you can. What do you think?

Your hands tell you lots about the things you feel with them. Is the pizza hot? Does the baseball have a smooth cover? Is the paint wet? How cold is the pool water?

Those same hands tell all kinds of things about you. For example, what happens to your hands when you are angry? Your hands curl into fists! If you're pleased, you clap your hands. And if you're frightened or upset, your hands shake.

Sometimes a doctor will examine your hands. The color and feel of your skin and nails tells him something about your health. Police also get information about people from their hands. There are lots of lines on every person's fingertips and palms. Each person has his or her own pattern of lines. No two people's patterns are alike, except those of identical twins. Police make prints of people's fingertips and palms. If they find a hand print on a stolen car and they have a copy of that print in their files, they can identify the criminal.

But the kind of hand reading you're interested in is something different. You want to know about reading palms to tell about people and their future.

Look very carefully at your hands. Notice all the lines and bumps. They make your very own pattern. No one else's is the same. Palm readers think that the size of your hands, their shape, and the lines and bumps all have meaning. And they think that they can read these meanings and tell if you'll be rich, if you will travel, if you will marry, along with the many other things in your future.

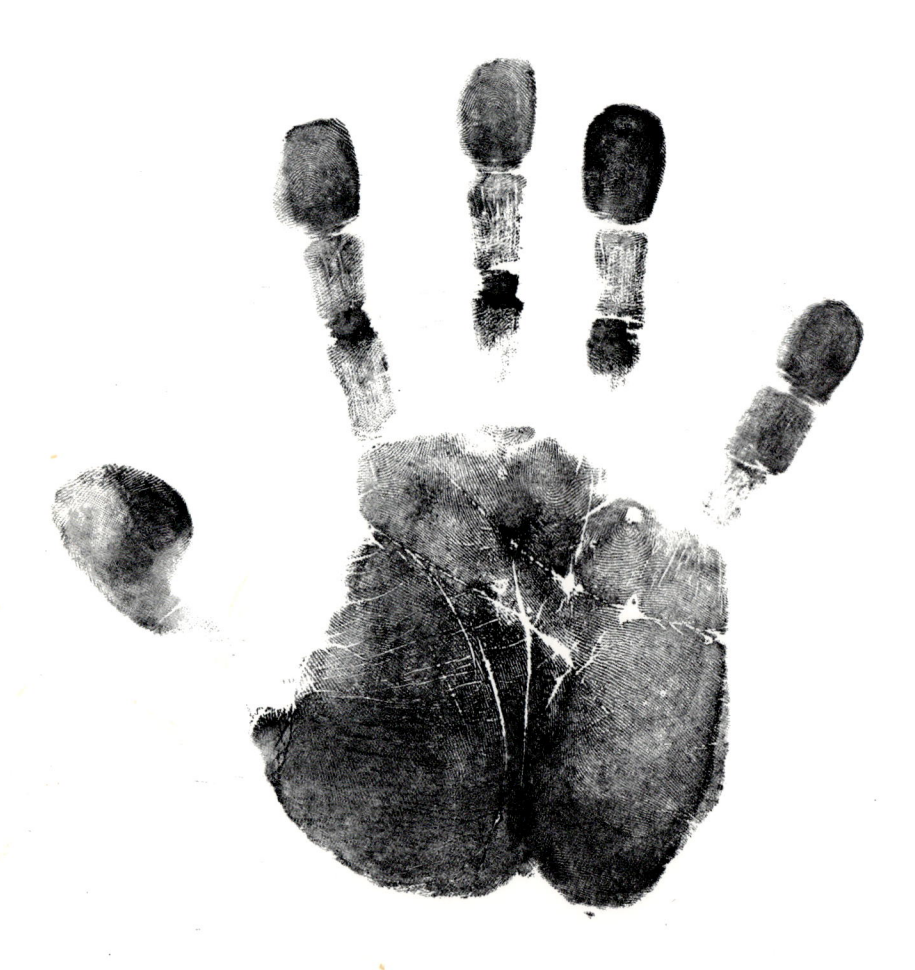

It is easier to read your palm if you make a print. All you need is an ink pad and two pieces of paper.

Palm readers often make prints of a person's hands to help them in a reading. You can make your own hand prints. All you need is an ink pad and two pieces of paper. Rub your hand (fingers and palm) all over the ink pad. Then press your hand against a piece of paper to make a print. Do the same with your other hand.

You will see lines of all kinds in the hand prints you made. The bumps in your hands will make dark spots. But what do these lines and bumps really mean? Which lines point to happiness? Which bumps tell of disaster?

The answers are really quite simple. All it takes is a little know-how and some imagination. Let's start by meeting some hands and getting to know them.

Meet Some Hands

Do you think both your hands are alike? They're not. One is really very different from the other. Are you left-handed or right-handed? Almost all hand readers believe you should study both, but they begin with the one you *don't* use for writing. They start with the left hand if you are right-handed. In palm reading, this is called the "less dominant" (the less strong) hand. On your ink prints, mark your less dominant hand.

This hand is like a map of your basic personality. It shows whether you are shy or like to talk

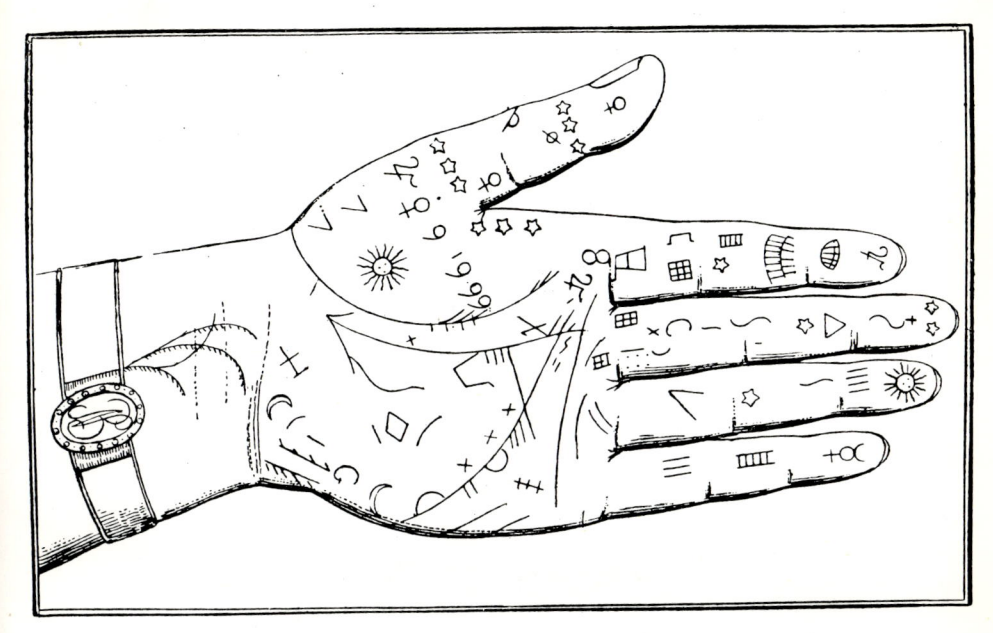

Napoleon Bonaparte's left hand, as sketched by a palm reader.

with everyone you meet. It tells whether you can stick to a job and do it carefully, or if you would rather have someone else do it. The other hand—the "active" hand—tells the palm reader if you are really doing what the first hand shows or if you are changing. *In palm reading, one hand always knows what the other is doing!*

How do your hands feel when people shake hands with you? Some hands may be like wet noodles—all soft and mushy. Their owners probably worry a lot. Other hands may be limp—they're often called "dead fish hands." That's because they are cold and heavy. They probably belong to people who are afraid of many things. Some people shake your hand so firmly that your hand feels numb. They are probably people who just don't want to go unnoticed.

Are your hands large? Are they flat? Do your hands go with the rest of your body? A short person will most likely have smaller hands than a person six feet tall.

Large hands belong to people who can work with small things or in a small space. Most dentists and surgeons have big hands. Secretaries and people who work with figures also have large hands. The mechanic who repairs your family car probably has big hands. Large-handed persons like everything in its place and exactly right. They like to do things for themselves. *A large-handed person can probably find a missing contact lens in a shaggy carpet!*

People with small hands like to work with big ideas and even bigger projects. They soon get bored and lose interest if a project has too many steps. They would be the first to plan a party, select the guests, and choose the menu. But small-handed party-givers are the last to write the invitations and cook the food. Small-handed people are likely to have messy desks, where large-handed people place every item in its own place.

In many cases, people have one hand that is smaller than the other. When the dominant hand is large and the active one is small, their owner learns things quickly but often carelessly.

Which hands do you think the president of your club or the manager of your team has—large or small? Right!—they're probably small.

But the size of your hand is only a part of the story. Your fingers tell a lot more about you.

Let Your Fingers Do the Talking!

Palm readers don't count thumbs as fingers. Thumbs are special, and we will look at them later. Meanwhile, that leaves four fingers to study.

Shake your hands a few times so they feel nice and loose. Then place them on a blank sheet of paper. Lay them on the paper in a way that feels comfortable. Ask a friend to make a tracing of your hands.

Remember when you study your hands to read the less dominant one first. That hand tells what you're basically like. Then read the active hand. It tells how your personality is changing as you go through life.

Now look at the tracings that were drawn. Are your fingers close together or even touching? That means you can keep a secret. It also means you probably save your allowance. If all of the fingers have large spaces between them, you're the type that lets money "fall through your fingers." But you usually spend it on other people. The large spaces between your fingers also show that you like to ask a lot of questions.

If your first finger (don't count your thumb!) and middle finger are the only ones with a large space between them, you like to plan and dream. But you often don't do what you set out to do. When the space is only between your third and fourth fingers, you often do things without thinking. *You're probably guilty of doing the wrong homework assignment, or maybe wearing one blue and one brown sock!*

The palm reader has a name for each finger. These names are for ancient gods and goddesses who supposedly watched over each finger.

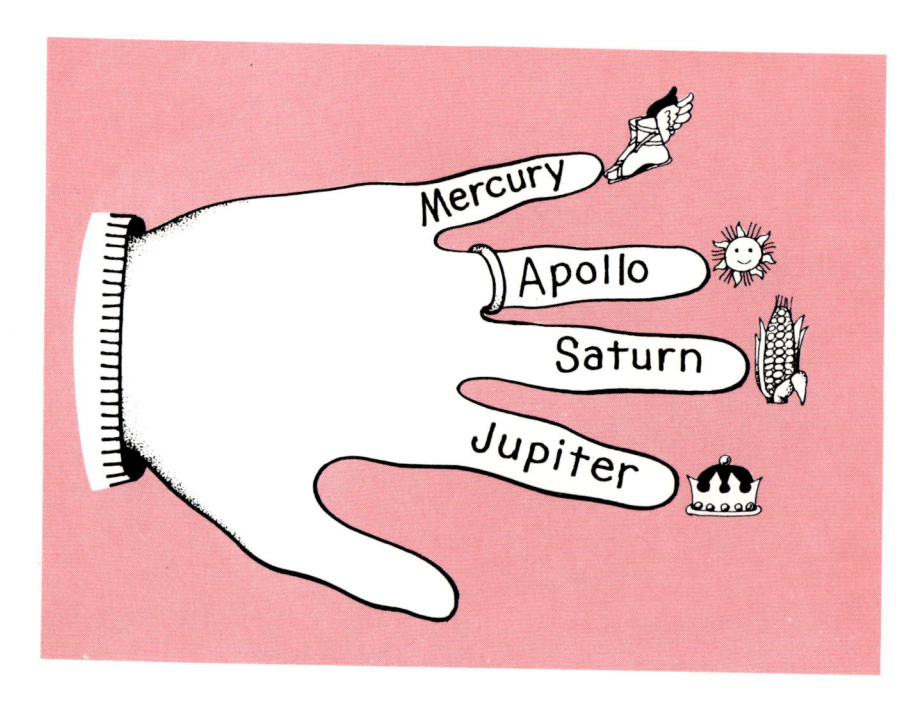

The first finger—the pointer—is named Jupiter, for the king of gods. You shake and point that finger when you want someone to listen to you. The middle finger is called Saturn, for the god of farming. This finger stands for usefulness and careful thinking. Doctors should have very strong Saturn fingers.

Apollo, the Sun god, gave his name to the ring finger. Apollo looked after the people who made or created things. Artists, writers, and musicians have strong Apollo fingers. The little finger is called Mercury, for the god of messages and quick thinking. Actors and people who sell things have strong Mercury fingers.

Saturn is the longest finger on most people. When it is straight and smooth, you are a person who needs to be alone to think. It also means you like to help people by doing useful things, like doing the dishes even when it's not your turn. If your Saturn finger is thin—and you are not a very thin person—you could become a scientist.

If your Jupiter finger (pointer) is tall and straight, it means you are ambitious and can make yourself do almost anything. The long Jupiter finger is the sign of the *leader*.

Why not check your class president's Jupiter finger. Is it tall and straight? When this finger is short, you are a good follower. If the bottom section of the Jupiter finger (the part that joins the rest of your hand) is thick and round, you are a good cook and like good food. If the middle of the finger is also strong, you are good at mathematics. (But that doesn't mean you *like* it!)

Now look at Apollo (the ring finger). If Apollo stands tall enough to reach the middle part of Saturn's nail, you like to entertain and amuse people. You do things for attention. And you get a lot of it.

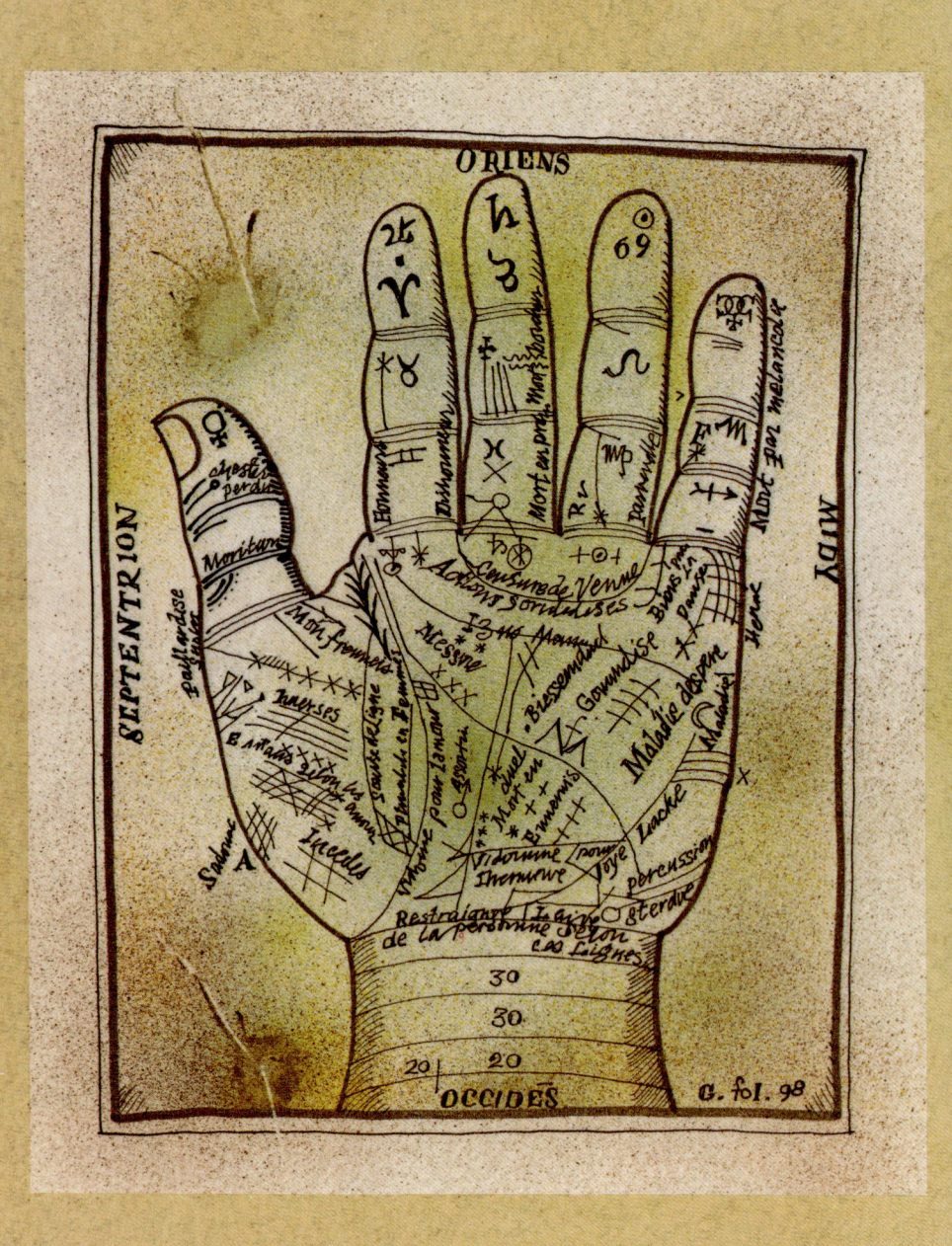

The art of palm reading developed over many centuries. Each part of the hand was given a particular symbol or name.

Look at the bottom of your Mercury finger (the smallest one). Is it lower than the bottom of the others? If so, you are shy, even though you may try to hide it. If Mercury is long, reaching to the top section of Apollo, you work and talk easily with other people. On some hands, the Mercury finger is twisted, just a little. This crooked finger belongs to a clever or sly person. *Beware of crooked Mercuries!*

There are three parts to each finger, divided by lines. Palm readers say that the top section stands for your mind. The middle section has to do with usefulness, and the lower section with your feelings. Which section on your fingers is the largest? The largest section tells what really controls your life. Are you a thinker, a doer, or a feeler?

This leaves us with one finger we have not studied—the thumb. This mystery finger holds the key to our choices. Believe it or not, your life may be ruled by your thumb!

Thumbs Up

Did you know that your thumb is the most important finger on your hand? Just try to pick up a glass of soda or a baseball bat without using your thumb. You'll find it difficult, to say the least! When you hurt your thumb and can't use it, you discover how hard it is to do even the simplest things with your hands. The all-important thumb can tell you a lot about its owner's personality.

Make a fist with the hand you do not use for writing. That's the less dominant one—remember? Look to see where your thumb is placed in the fist. Is it under the rest of

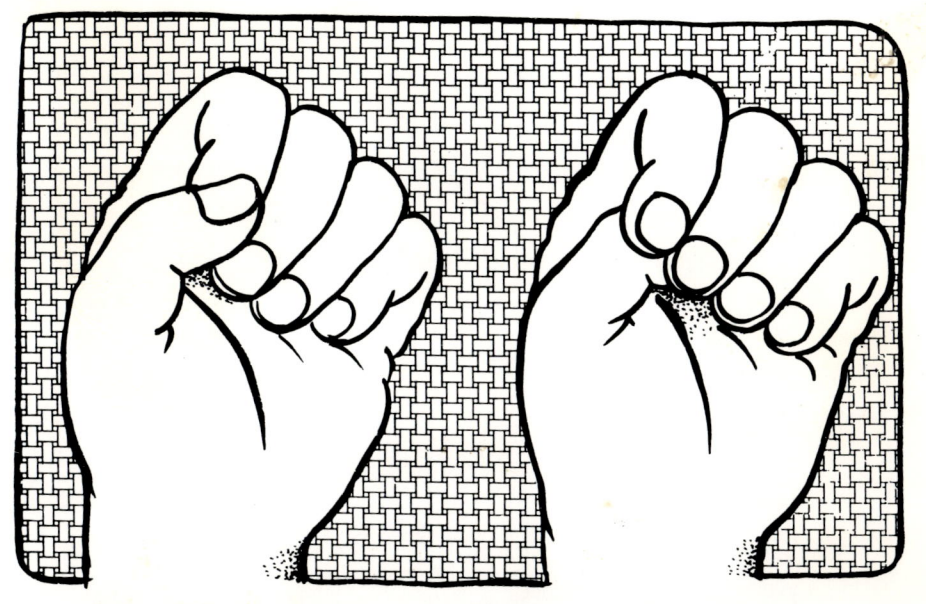

Make a fist. If your thumb rests on top of your fingers, you are strong-willed and easily angered. If it is hidden, you may be unsure of yourself.

your fingers, or is it on top of them? If it's hidden under the fingers, you are still learning to be sure of yourself. Sometimes you are uncomfortable with other people. You would rather do things with one or two friends than with a big group. You need to know that your family and friends love you.

If the thumb is on top of the fingers, you like to be on top of things. You have to be right in everything you do. And you're easily angered. You try not to let your feelings show, but sometimes that is hard.

Now look at the lower part of your thumb. Is it straight and thick, or does it seem to curve in? If it is thick and straight, you are a person who makes decisions without looking for reasons. Sometimes this is called "using intuition." When you decide to start an airplane model, you'll paint all the pieces, attach all the emblems, stick on the propeller, *and then remember you don't have the glue!*

When you make up your mind about what you want to do, all the reasons your friends or family give you will not change your mind. Some people may even call you "stubborn."

If your lower thumb curves in like an hourglass, then you like to think before you make decisions. You practice the slogan "Look before you leap." You're not the type to try out for the skating team without taking lessons for six months. If your thumb is thick with no curve, you don't think about whether you're ready. You just sign up for the team because it "feels" good.

Is your thumb long or short? (A long thumb measures halfway up the bottom section of your pointer.) People with short thumbs are dreamers and like to be told what to do. Those who have long thumbs like to give directions.

Your thumb has a strong effect on the other fingers. For example, a strong Apollo (ring finger) means an interest in music, reading, and art. But the *kind* of interest depends on your thumb. If the thumb is *long*, it means you may want to play music. But if the thumb is *short*, you would rather listen to it. Long thumbs belong to people who do things.

The size and shape of fingers are very important in palm reading. Did you know that square fingers and nails belong to people who don't like to use their imaginations? And that flat fingers usually belong to presidents? Could it be that what we become can depend on what our fingers look like?

The Shape of Things

Palms and fingers come in different shapes and sizes. Long palms belong to *thinkers* and short ones to *doers*. What they think about or do (and how much) depends on the rest of the hand.

Do you have short, square palms and short fingers? Then you probably follow the rules wherever you are—at home, in school, or on a job. When you ride a bicycle, you stop at signs and red lights. You don't daydream very much, and you don't plan ahead. But if your palm is square and your fingers are long, you think as well as act on things. You like rules, but you think about how best to use them. It may mean you would make a good lawyer or referee.

But maybe your palm is long with short fingers. If so, you like to travel, and you form ideas very much on your own. You tell people what *you* think, but sometimes you don't listen to *their* ideas. If your palm and fingers are both long (and that means you have a big hand), then you like to work with ideas and details. You probably enjoy history and science.

While palms have two shapes—square and long—fingers have four different shapes. Look at the tips of your fingers—the parts that carry the fingernails. What is the shape of your fingertips? (Most of the time, fingertips and nails have the same shape.)

The first shape to look for in a fingertip is a *square*. Square fingers and square nails often belong to people who don't like change. "We always do it this way," they often say. These people will have one, and only one, way of doing things. *There is little you can do to budge a "square finger."*

The second shape has a special name, *spatulate*. It is the shape of a pancake turner or a spatula in the kitchen. Some people describe it as "spade-shaped." Spatulate fingers and nails are wider at the top than at the bottom. This is the finger shape of a thinker. If often means you are a doer, as well. If you have spatulate fingers, or at least three spatulate nails, you probably have loads of energy.

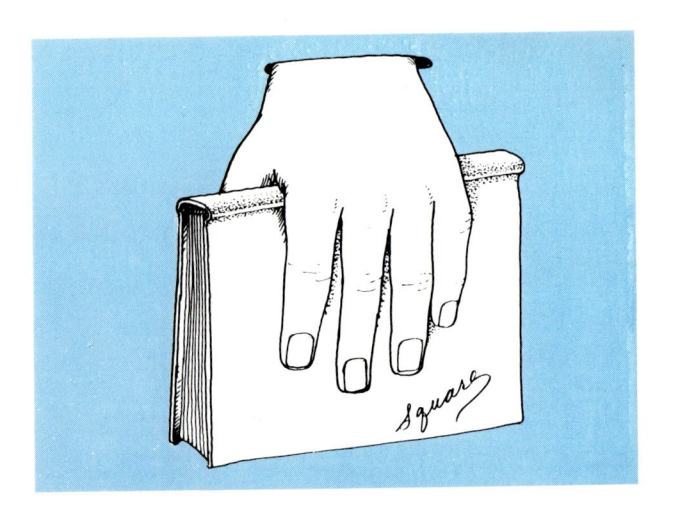

A spatulate Jupiter finger (pointer) means you might become a leader in business or in sports. A spatula shaped finger and nail on Saturn (middle finger) shows you'll make a good manager. Almost all our presidents had spatulate shaped fingers and nails.

A spatulate shape on an Apollo (ring finger) usually belongs to a house painter or a clothes designer. On Mercury fingers (pinky), this shape belongs to people who like to talk about useful things, like TV weather forecasters.

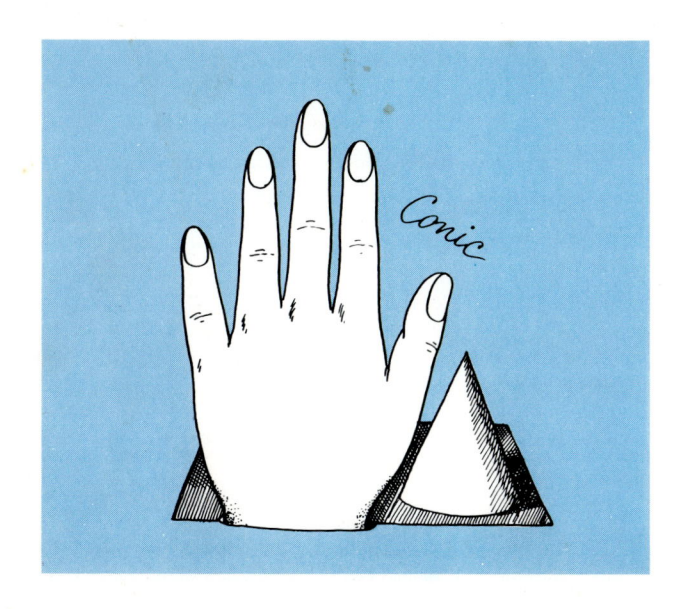

The third shape looks like a cone and is called *conic*. It's a little wider at the bottom of the fingertip than at the tip itself. Conic shapes are usually on small hands—these people like to plan and lead and think. People with conic fingers and nails can't seem to hold on to things. They must be very careful, for example, not to break dishes when they wash them.

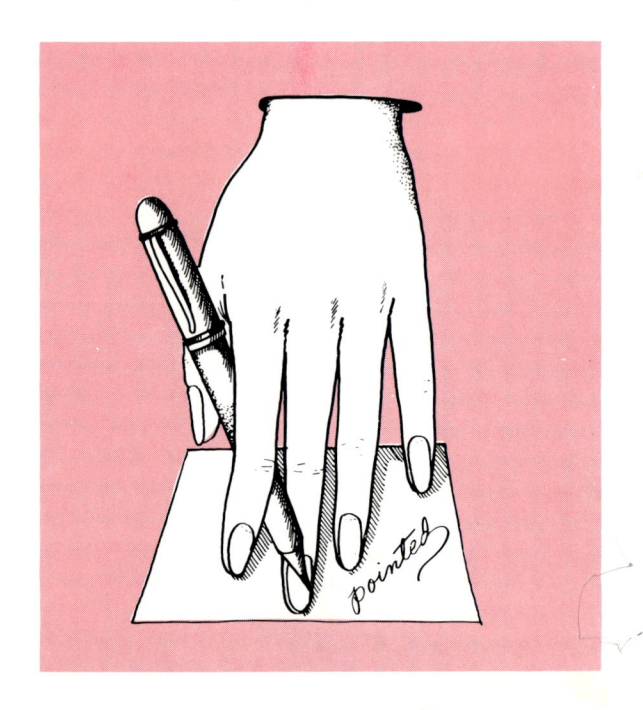

The managers of sports teams and other leaders will often have conic nails on pointer fingers. Is your middle finger conic? If so, you're the type to keep changing the furniture around in your room. When the tip of your ring finger looks like a cone, it means you like to write poetry or your own music. You may become a rock star. If the tip of your little finger is conic, then your imagination works overtime. *Tall tales should really interest you.*

The last fingertip shape is *pointed.* These fingers and nails are long and thin. They are considered the most attractive. Models use their pointed fingers and nails in TV commercials. People with pointed fingers and nails are often not practical. They need someone to show them how to make good use of their skills and energy. The pointed finger needs advice and direction.

CHAPTER 7

On to the Palms

It was almost 10:30 at night when Jennifer realized she was alone with Aunt Kate. They had talked all evening. One by one, the rest of the family had quietly yawned their way to bed. No one had bothered to say good night. They knew it would have gone unheard by the young girl and her wise, soft-spoken aunt.

Jennifer couldn't remember when she had enjoyed an evening more. Aunt Kate had read Jennifer's palm print for her and they had explored Jennifer's personality using her hand tracing and the shapes and sizes of her fingers. While there were some things she thought were not true about herself, Jennifer had to admit that there *were* certain things about her that Aunt Kate could not have known without somehow reading them in her hands that evening.

Jennifer found herself feeling the way so many of us feel about things we don't understand. "I want to believe it all because my Aunt Kate does," she thought. "She really did find out a lot of things about me but there is so much about this that doesn't seem real or *possible*."

Suddenly, Aunt Kate appeared to be reading her thoughts because she said, "Jennifer, this must all be a bit strange for you. I mean, how can I expect someone to believe that so much about them is written in their hands? No, don't try to tell me you have become a believer in so short a time. No one should make his or her mind up about palm reading until they have lots of evidence for or against it. It's very important to make up your own mind about such things."

Aunt Kate took Jennifer's hand in her own, turned the child's hand palm up, and looked at it for a few seconds. "Now, young lady, for your final lesson—*how to read a palm.*"

Life Lines and Head Lines

There are messages in your palms that are easy to read when you know how. Look at the many lines in your own palm. If you look at the palm of your less dominant hand, you will probably find more lines than on the other hand.

Some people have palm lines that are very deep and easy to see. To the palm reader, these are people with strong opinions and very deep feelings about things. They *like* something, or they *hate* it. Seldom do they feel "in-between" about things.

The palm lines of a calm, relaxed person are usually clear and unbroken—there are few shorter branches coming from the longer lines. When the lines are very branched, however, the palm reader feels the person is troubled and may have difficulties. The palm with "scratchy" looking lines that go every which way belongs to a person who lacks energy. The palm that has lines in regular patterns belongs to the active person with lots of energy.

There are three main lines the palm reader looks for—the *life line,* the *head line,* and the *heart line.* Some people do not have all of them. The lines are thought to change all through life. Even on the same hand, they are sometimes easy to see while, at other times, they seem to almost disappear. The main palm lines may move from one area of the palm to another. They may also change in size during a lifetime.

The first line to look for is the *life line.* It begins between the thumb and the pointer finger. It curves upward toward your wrist. Sometimes it will fork and spread into two or more directions. Each part of the fork is called a branch. If a branch moves toward the little finger, you will travel a lot in your lifetime. When another branch goes toward your thumb,

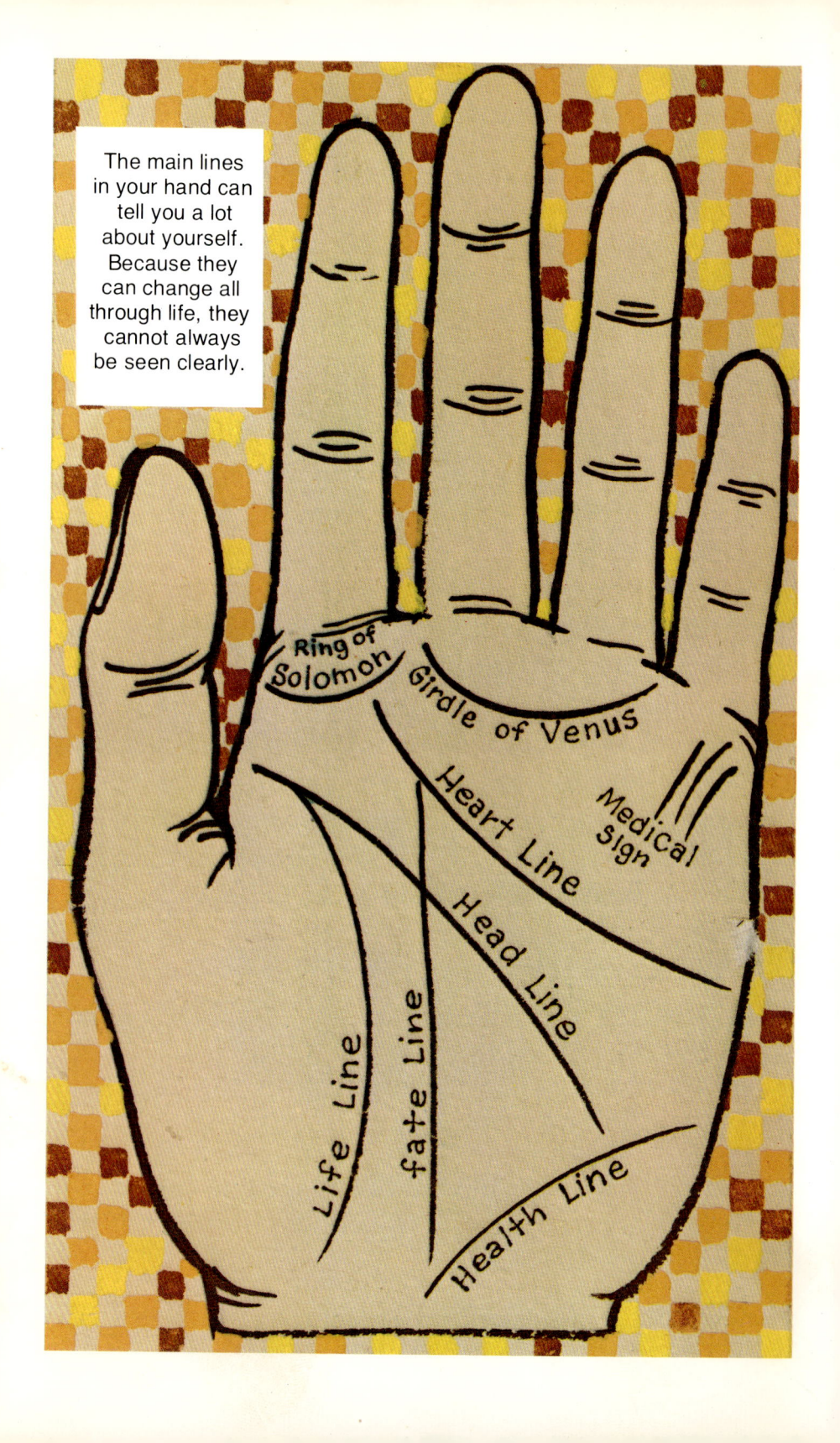

The main lines in your hand can tell you a lot about yourself. Because they can change all through life, they cannot always be seen clearly.

- Ring of Solomon
- Girdle of Venus
- Heart Line
- Medical Sign
- Head Line
- Life Line
- Fate Line
- Health Line

you will stay close to your family even if you do travel.

The life line has nothing to do with how long you will live. The length of the life line only shows how much physical energy you have. A long, deep line, easy to see, shows that you have lots of energy and "push." A short line, or a line that is hard to see, means you need a lot of rest. *Check this line after a week of track practice!*

Some life lines look more like chains than smooth lines. To the palm reader, such a hand belongs to a "worrier" or someone who often doesn't "feel well." You've heard of people who "worry themselves sick." Breaks in the life line show changes. Perhaps you will move to another neighborhood or change schools. A break in the life line may also mean a narrow escape from a serious accident.

The *head line* begins in one of two places. First, it may start with the life line. Very soon it separates and moves across toward the center of the palm. It may begin above the life line, so that there is a space between them. Then it moves toward the center of your palm.

The head line has to do with the way a person thinks. When it is joined to the start of the life line, the palm belongs to a planner. If it starts above the life line, it is on the palm of someone who does things with no particular plan—someone who just "feels like doing them."

If the head line moves almost straight across the hand, the palm reader knows the mind rules the heart. The palm belongs to someone who wants all the figures and facts before doing anything. When the head line bends a bit, we have a person who wants to work with facts but will consider new ideas. The more it curves, the more new things the person will like to think about. If it curves all the way to the little finger, the palm reader sees a person who lives in his or her own world.

The length of the head line shows how many things you can think about at the same time. If the line is deep and long, we have someone who thinks about many things. If it is short or hard to see, we have someone who finds it hard to concentrate.

The third most important line is the *heart line*—the topmost line of the palm, under the fingers. In some hands, the head line and heart

The space between the head line and the life line is called "the angle of luck." If the space is wide, as it is in the picture, you are very lucky.

Not everyone has a solar line—the double lines shown in the picture. But if you do, it might give you fame.

41

line are joined into one. The palm reader feels this hand belongs to people who are confused and trying to decide whether to listen to their feelings or to their thoughts. These people also want to be the center of attention.

The heart line starts somewhere under the pinky and moves across the hand toward the pointer. The shorter it is, the more suspicious is the person about other people. If it goes as far as the space between the middle finger and the pointer, it belongs to someone who likes, and is liked by, others.

The palm reader believes that if lots of lines branch from the heart line, it is the hand of someone who will love many times. If the line is chained, there may be many problems in love.

Sometimes there may be some special marks or lines in your hand that are *special* messages. You will not find all of these in every hand. Some hands won't have any. Remember—everyone is different and every hand is different. That's what makes them fun to read.

The *fate line* begins below the wrist and moves toward the fingers. It is in the middle of the hand. If it is long, approaching a finger, its owner has a good chance to succeed. When it makes a triangle with the head line and life line, it means good luck.

Look at the pad under your little finger. Do you see at least three lines running up and down? These lines are called the *medical sign*. No, it doesn't mean you will become a doctor or a nurse. It means you may help people feel good.

Once in a while you will find a small curved line on the pad under the pointer finger. This is called the *ring of Solomon*. See if you have one on your palm. Solomon was a very wise king in the Bible. If you have the ring of Solomon, you understand mysterious, unusual things.

The pad under your ring finger has a special meaning. If you see three up and down lines there, the palm reader will tell you your pockets will never be empty. Even if you spend all your money, some more will always come.

Another mark to look for is the *Girdle of Venus*. This is a short line curving from the ring finger to the pointer. Many hands have only a part of this line. To the palm reader, the longer the line, the more active its owner's imagination.

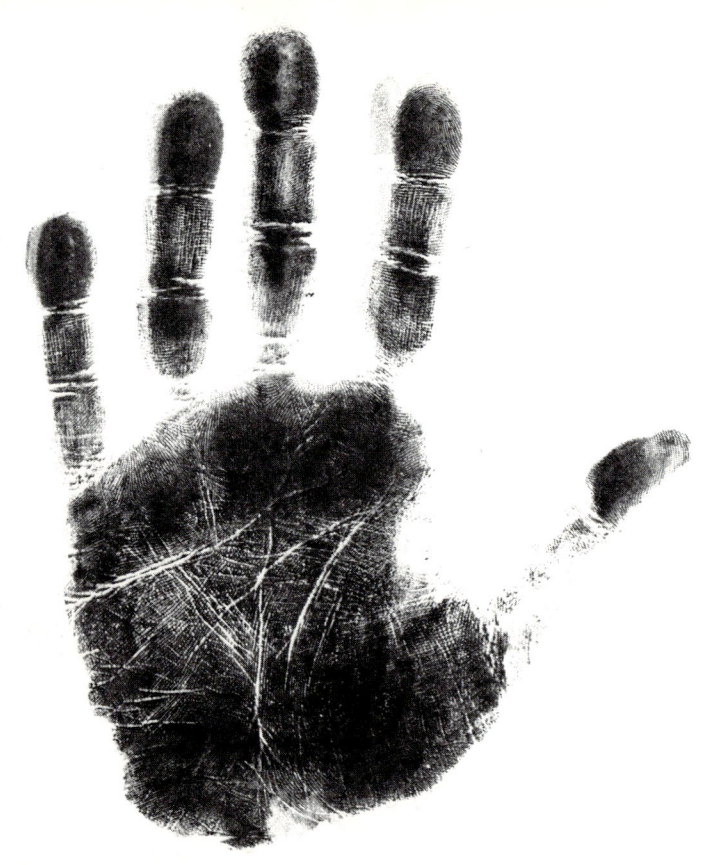

Here is Jennifer's palm print. You know enough now to read it. Write down what you can read from it about Jennifer and her future. Aunt Kate's reading is on page 48.

Stars, crosses, and "x"s often appear on palms. Stars mean successes. The crosses and "x"s foretell difficulties.

When your friends find out you can read palms, they will often ask the question: "Will I get married?" Ask them to bend their fingers to touch their palm. Then look at the side of the hand below the little finger. If you see a crossing line or two, that is said to mean the person will marry.

CHAPTER 9

The Unanswered Question

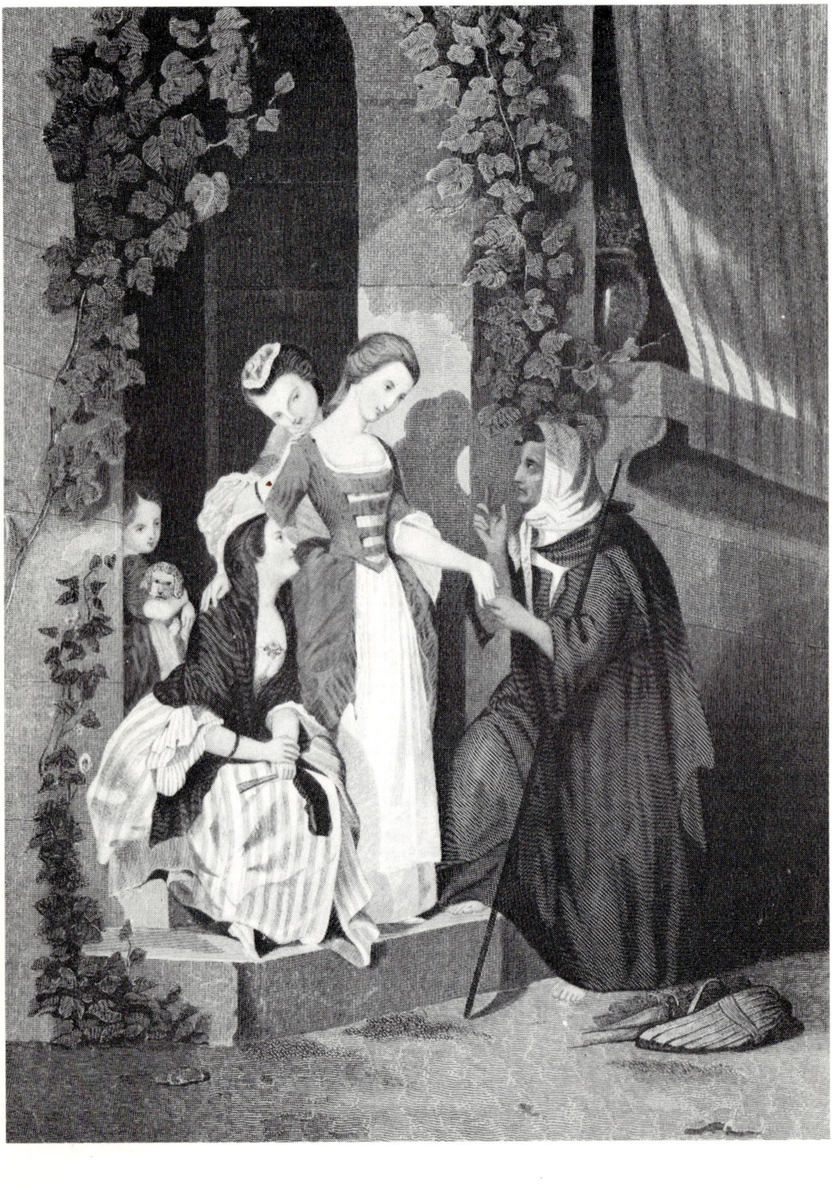

Jennifer hadn't realized the clock was chiming until she became aware there had been 12 bongs. Midnight! Where had the time gone? She wasn't the least bit tired. Would she be able to sleep at all tonight? She hoped so because the morning would come more quickly if she slept the night. And *this* morning she would be reading the palm of every friend she could find.

"Aunt Kate, even though I don't understand everything you talked about, I can see why you've had so much fun all your life!" Jennifer looked at her aunt, almost said something, but stopped herself.

"What's the matter, Jen?" Aunt Kate said gently. "Go on and say what's on your mind."

Jennifer smiled shyly. Then she looked straight into her aunt's eyes and said, "Aunt Kate, what if I *never really believe* that people can tell the future? Will that mean I can never do the things you have done?"

Aunt Kate smiled. She stretched her arms in the air, tired from the long evening together. "Jen, there are certainly as many people who don't believe in palm reading as there are people who do. All I can tell you is that palm readers, all through history, have warned kings of illness or death in battle. They predicted great heroes, and they have prevented crimes and disasters."

Jennifer's aunt started across the room, holding her niece's hand. Then, she turned toward the puzzled girl, chuckled, and said, "But Jen, if you really want the answer to your own future, you know where to find it. It's right there in the palm of your hand!"

Aunt Kate's Reading: Jennifer's life line shows she is strong and very enthusiastic. Her head line curves downward. That means Jennifer is very creative. If you look carefully, you'll see a line crossing the head line. This shows that Jennifer may be bothered by a problem she is having trouble solving. Jennifer's heart line is slightly curved and long. That says that Jennifer is a warm and loving person — really a romantic. Jennifer's fingers and nails are spatulate—spade shaped. These are the fingers of a thinker and doer. Jennifer has loads of energy. She'll probably grow up a dreamer, but one who puts ideas into action.

MALCOLM CAMPBELL HIGH SCHOOL
3400 NADON STREET

001.94　　　　　　　　　　　　　　22190
　H　　Hoffman, Elizabeth
　　　　Visions Of The Future:
　　　　Palm Reading

MALCOLM CAMPBELL HIGH SCHOOL
3400 NADON STREET
MONTREAL, QUEBEC H4J 1P5

MALCOLM CAMPBELL HIGH SCHOOL
3400 NADON STREET
MONTREAL, QUEBEC H4J 1P5